An International Princess Alphabet Primer

I0558768

Jenny Fulton

Illustrated by Olha Tkachenko

Copywrite © 2024 Jenny Fulton
International Princess Primers Series
All rights reserved.

Subject Matter:
JUVENILE NONFICTION/Concepts/Alphabet
JUVENILE NONFICTION/Girls & Women
JUVENILE NONFICTION/People & Places Other

Target Age:
Juvenile 0-12, Ages 3-6, Grade K-1

Illustrated by Olha Tkachenko with Little Big Me
Cover Design by Sonia Freitas with Chloe Belle Arts

Albuquerque, NM
heart-soul-mind.org
jennyannlitfin@gmail.com

Hardcover: 979-8-9856260-3-2
Paperback: 979-8-9856260-4-9
Ebook: 979-8-9856260-5-6

This book is for all the little princesses around the world, from every nation and culture, and to my little princesses, Chloe, Sophia, and Selah. You are beautiful, unique, and immeasurably precious.

Also dedicated to my teacher education instructors, Dr. Susan Alford and Dr. Michelle Lundgren, who inspired a love of creative, interactive teaching, encouraged my interest in cross-cultural environments, and traveled with me to my first full-time teaching job at an international school in China. Thank you for all your love and dedication.

Aa is for Alicorn.

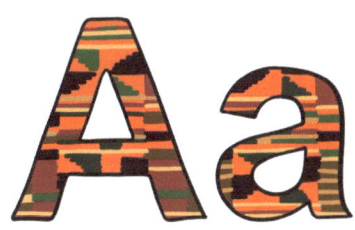

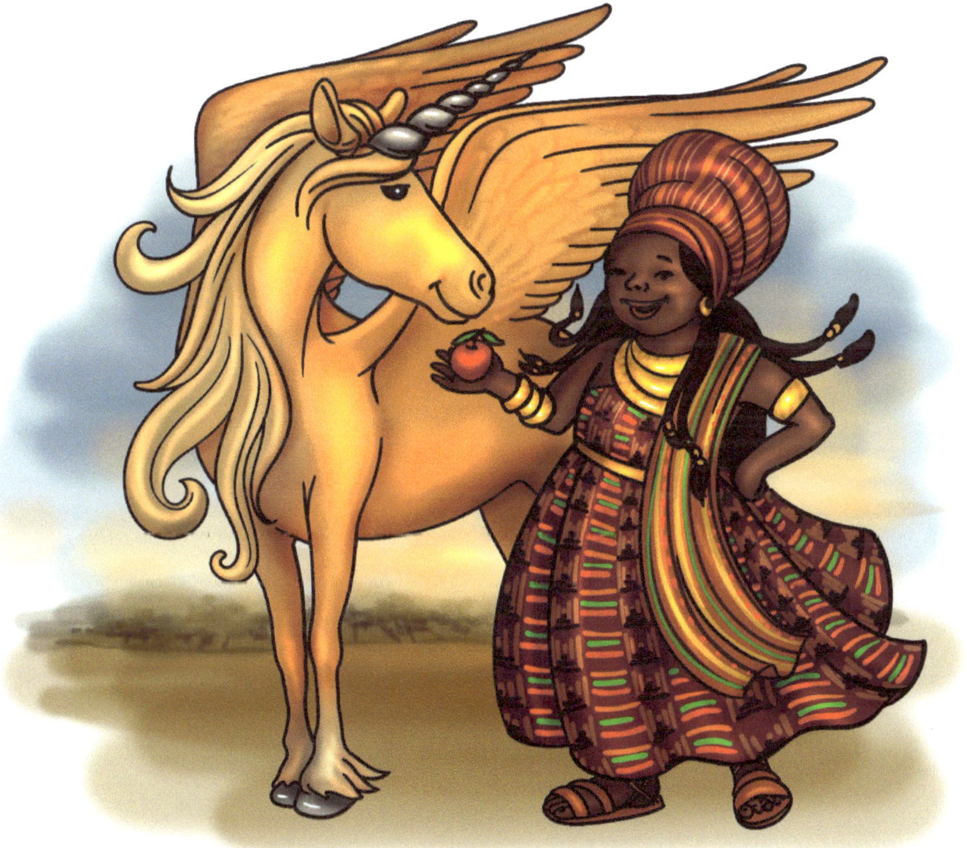

African Princess Amina

Bb is for Ballgown.

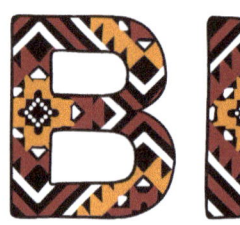

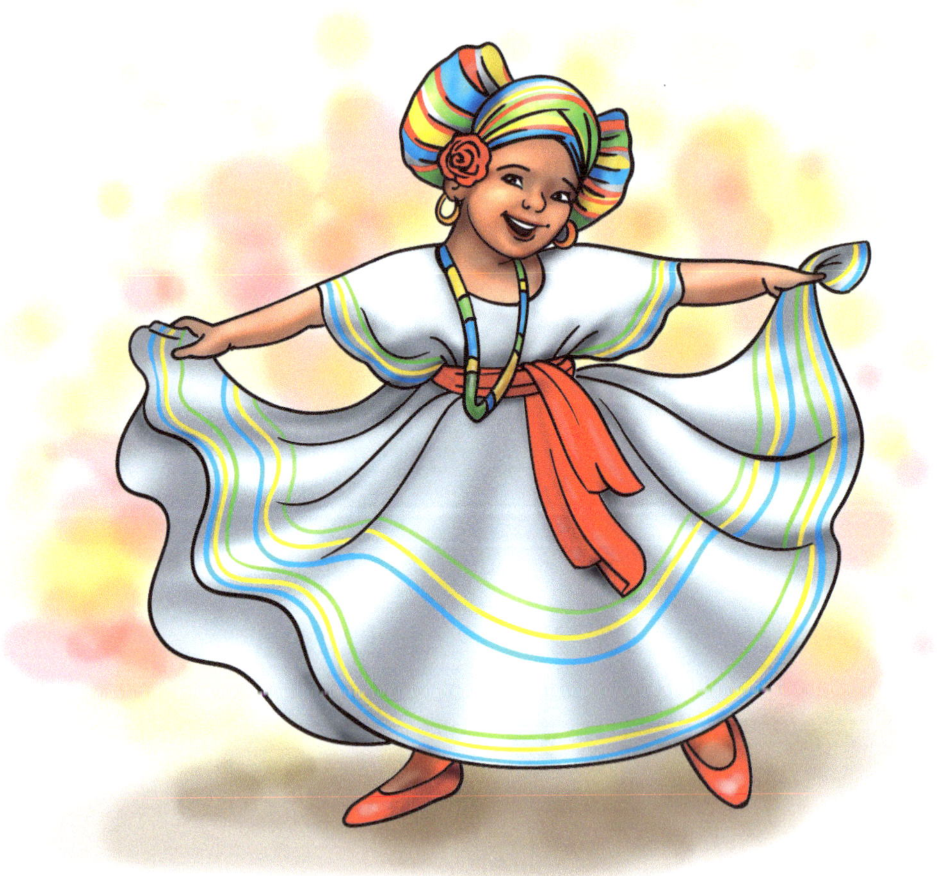

Brazilian Princess Isabel

Cc is for Castle.

Chinese Princess Changping

Dd is for Dragon.

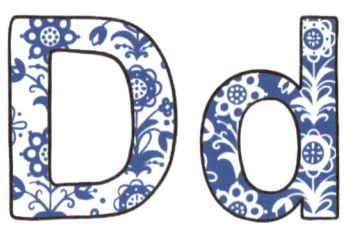

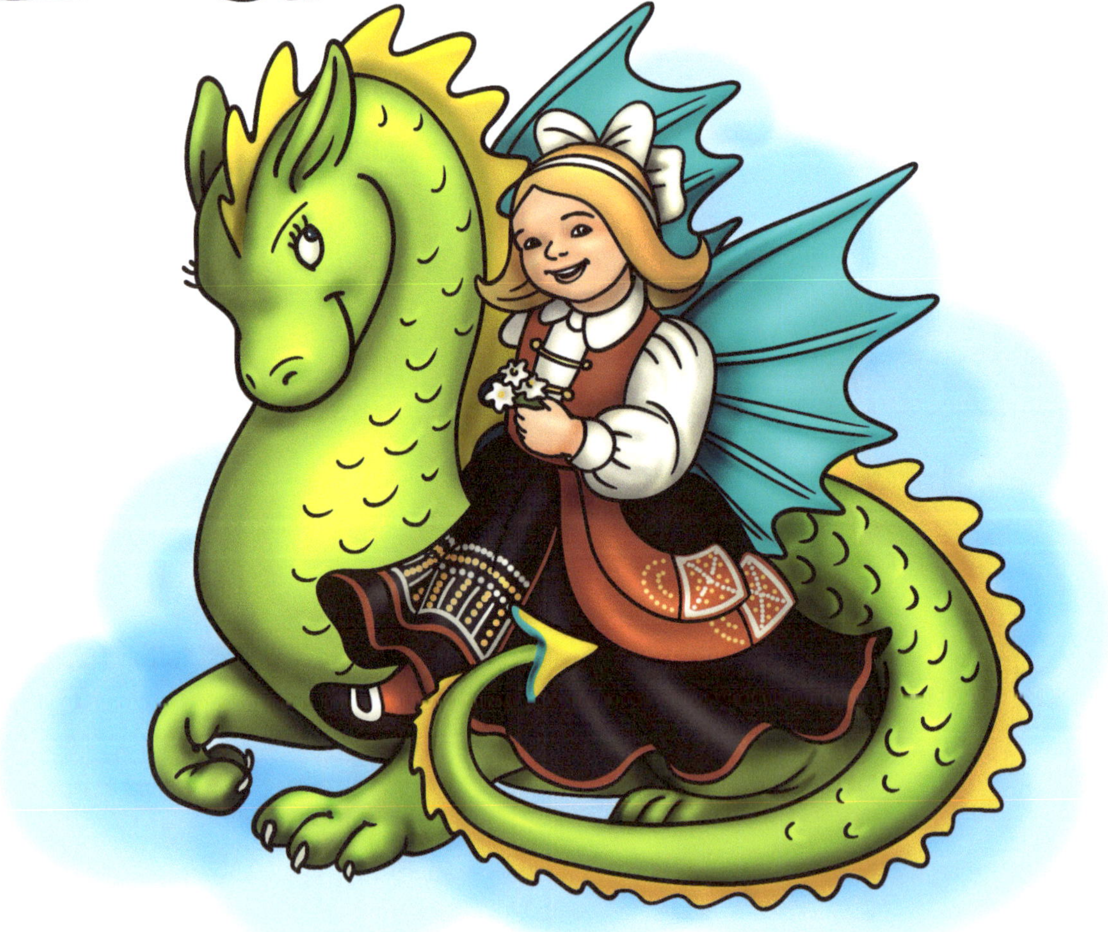

Danish Princess Sophie

Ee is for Elf.

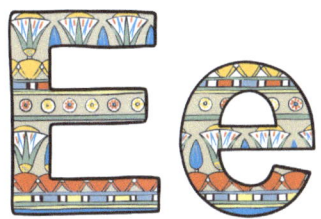

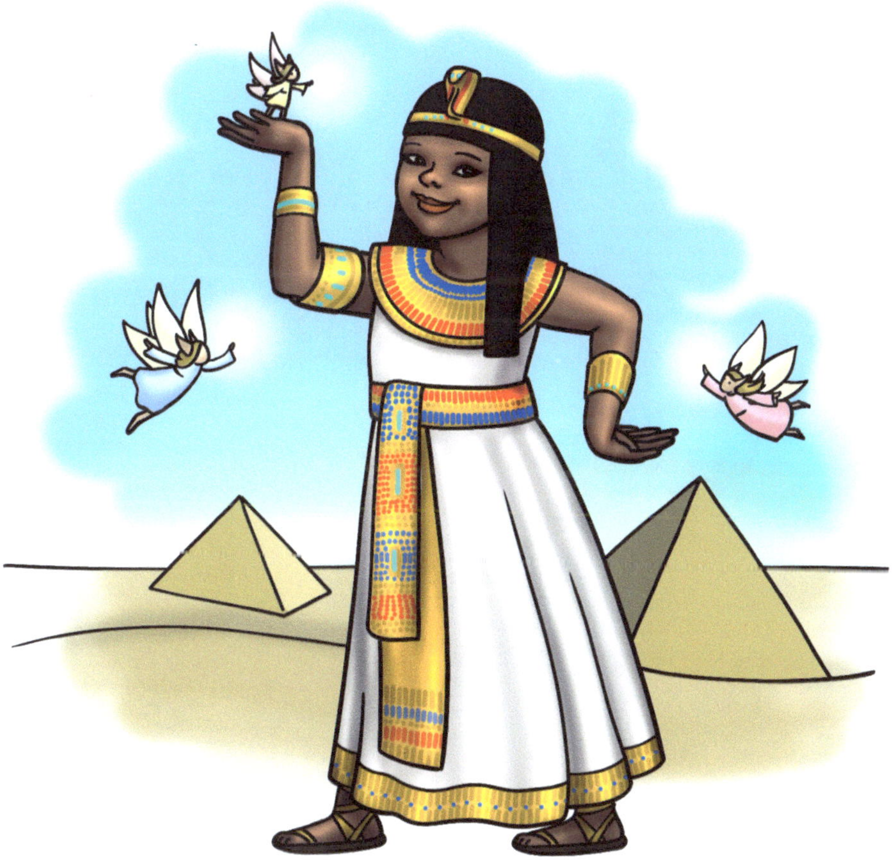

Egyptian Princess Cleopatra

 **is for Fairy.**

French Princess Eleanor

 **is for Giant.**

Guatemalan Princess Clara

Hh is for Hobgoblin.

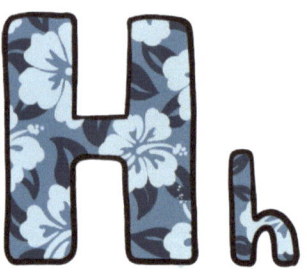

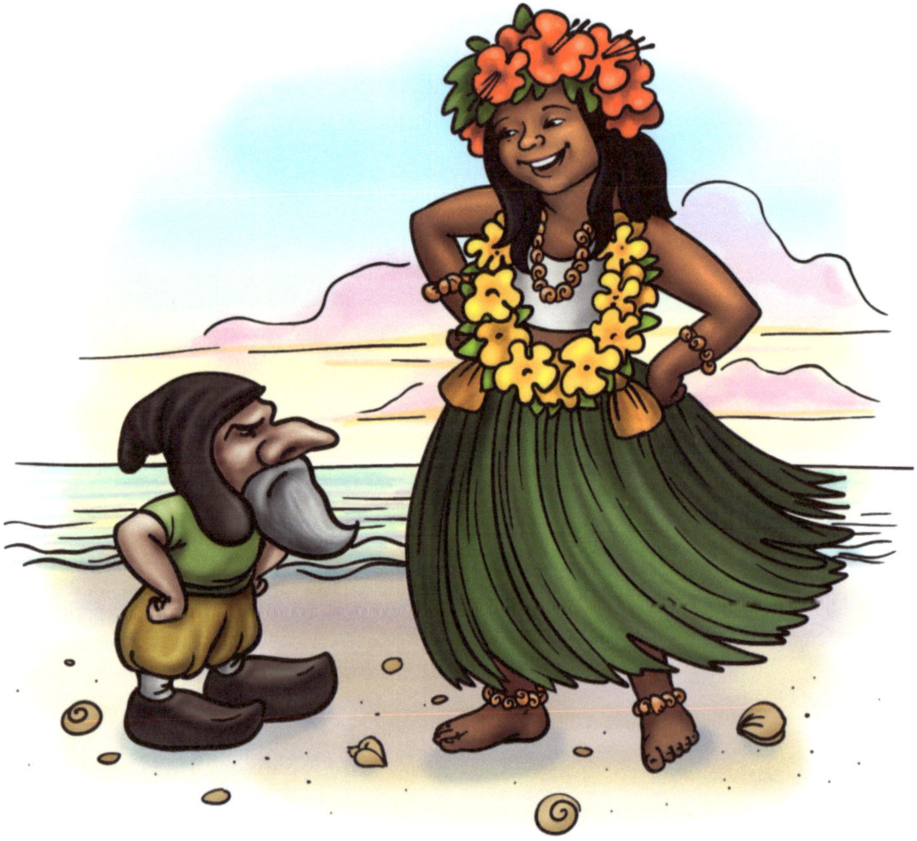

Hawaiian Princess Kaiulani

 is for Invisible.

Inuit Princess Mikak

 is for Jewels.

Jewish Princess Esther

Kk is for King.

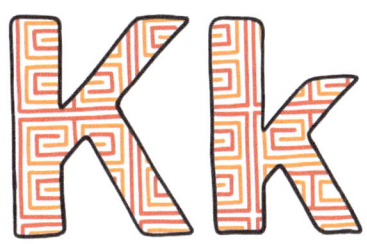

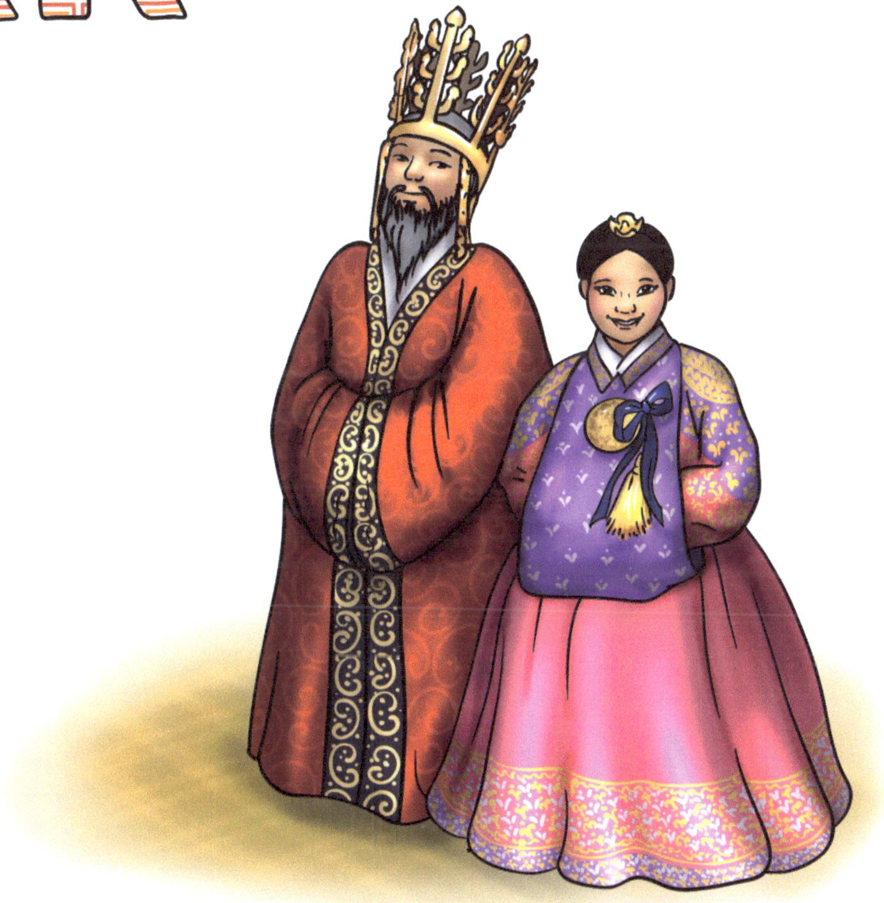

Korean Princess Deokon

 **is for Lion.**

Lithuanian Princess Aldona

Mm is for Mermaid.

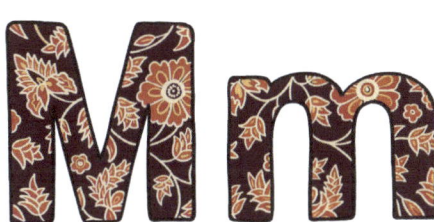

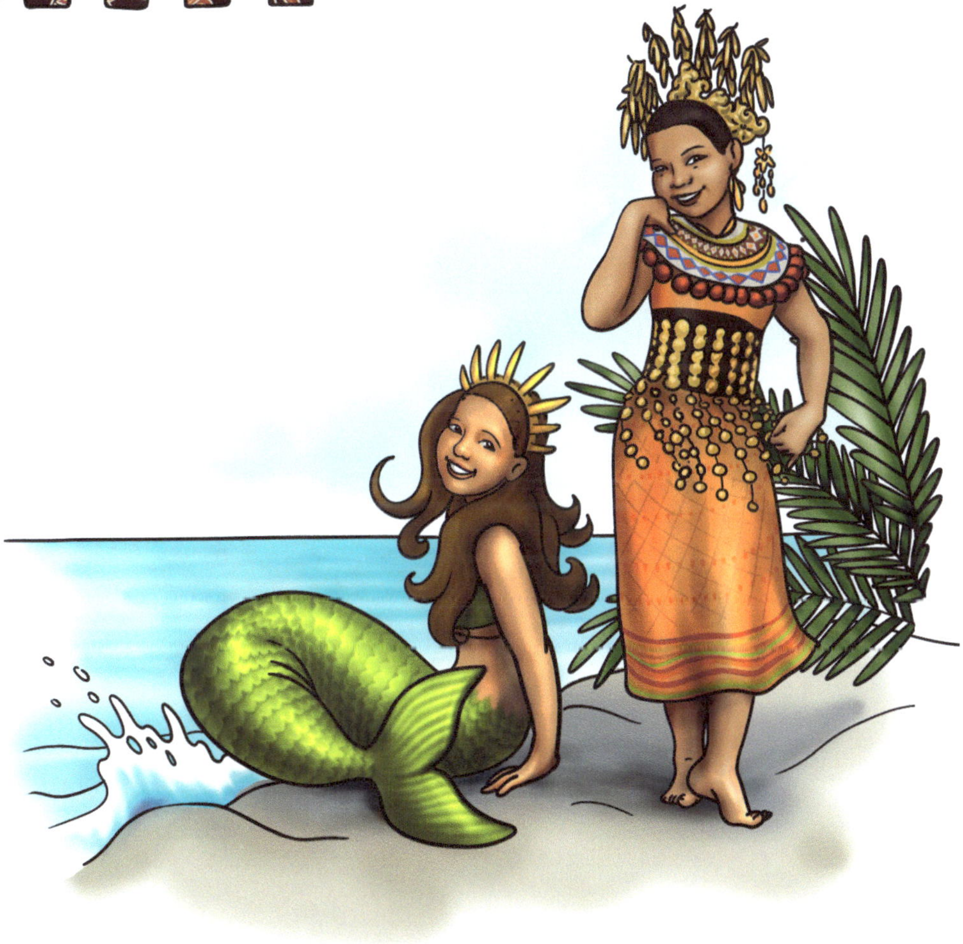

Malaysian Princess Puteri

Nn is for Nature.

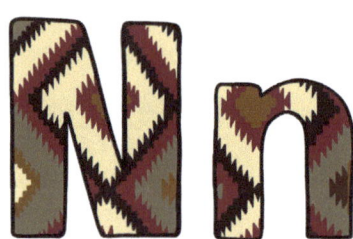

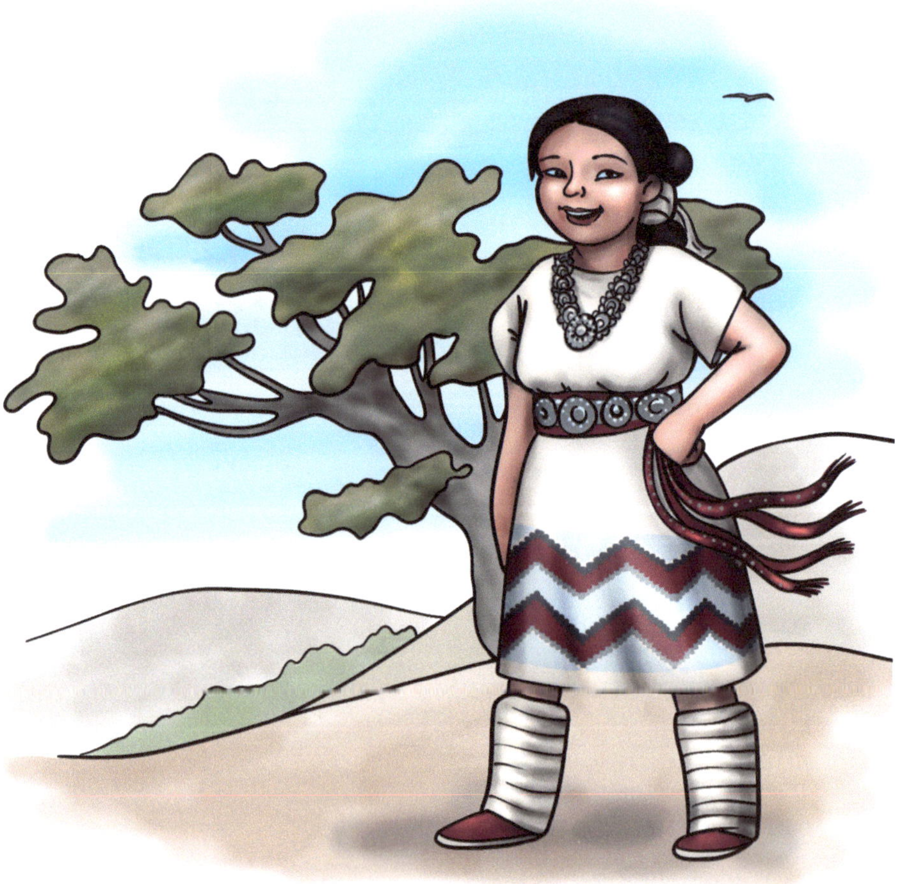

Navajo Princess Beulah

Oo is for Ogre.

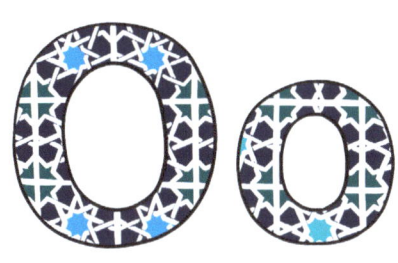

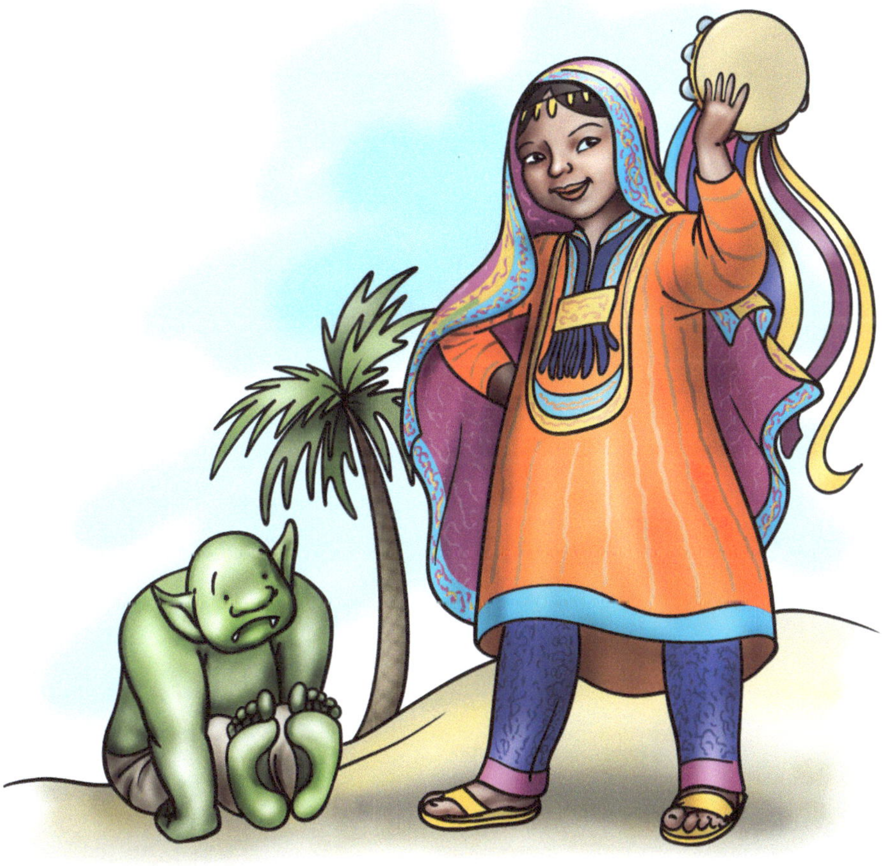

Omani Princess Sayyida

Pp is for Pegasus.

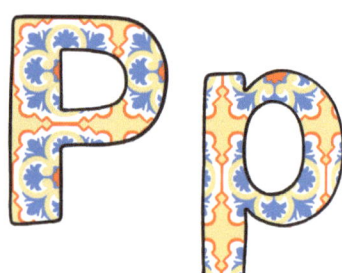

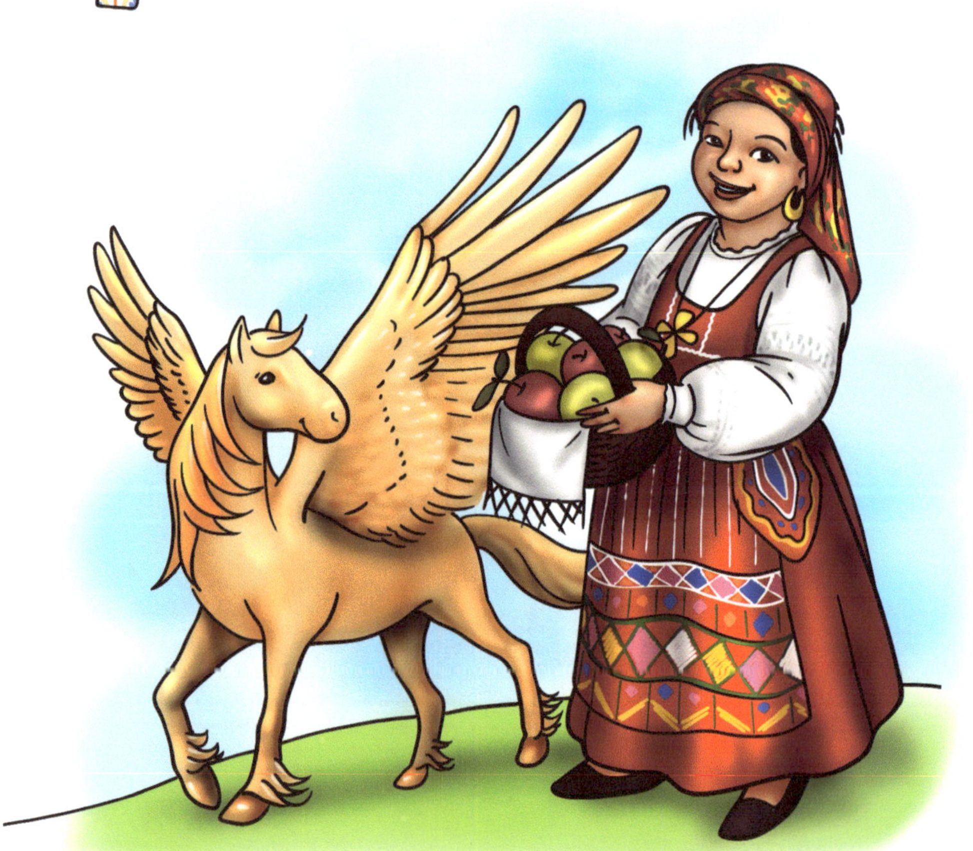

Portuguese Princess Catherine

Qq is for Queen.

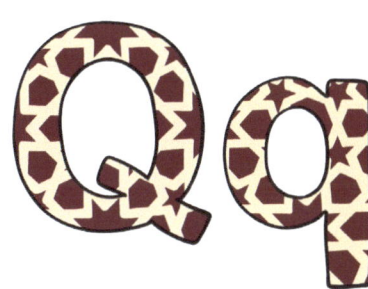

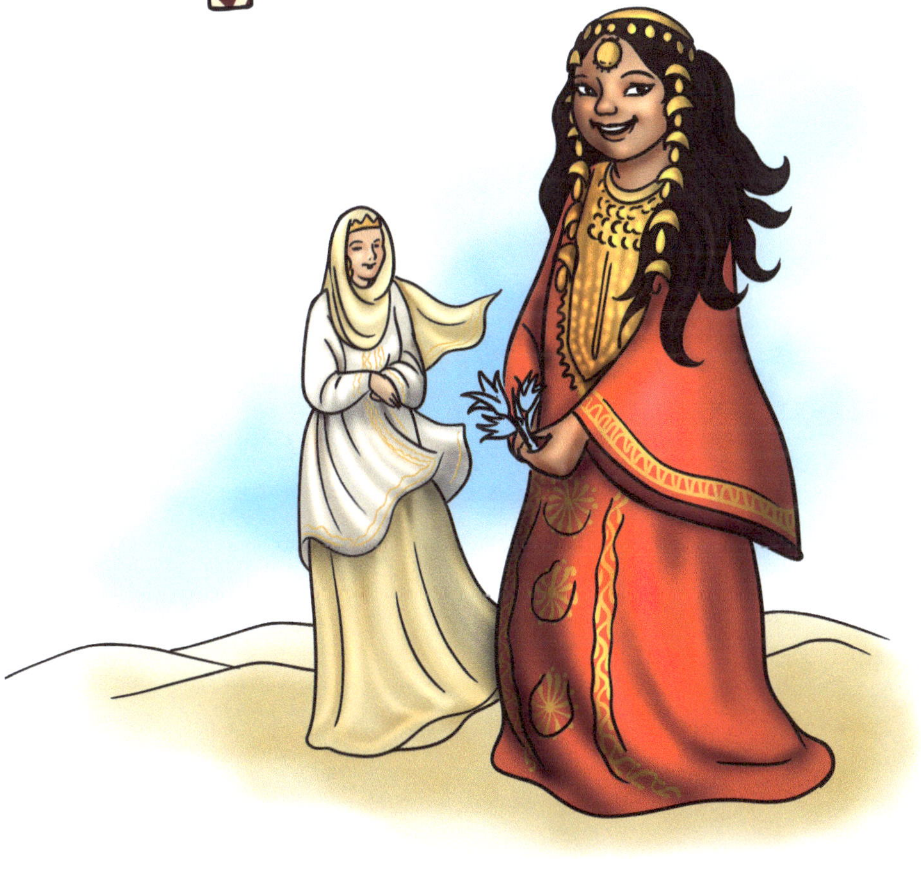

Qatari Princess Moza

Rr is for Ring.

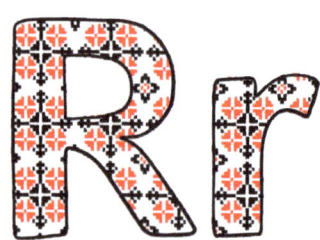

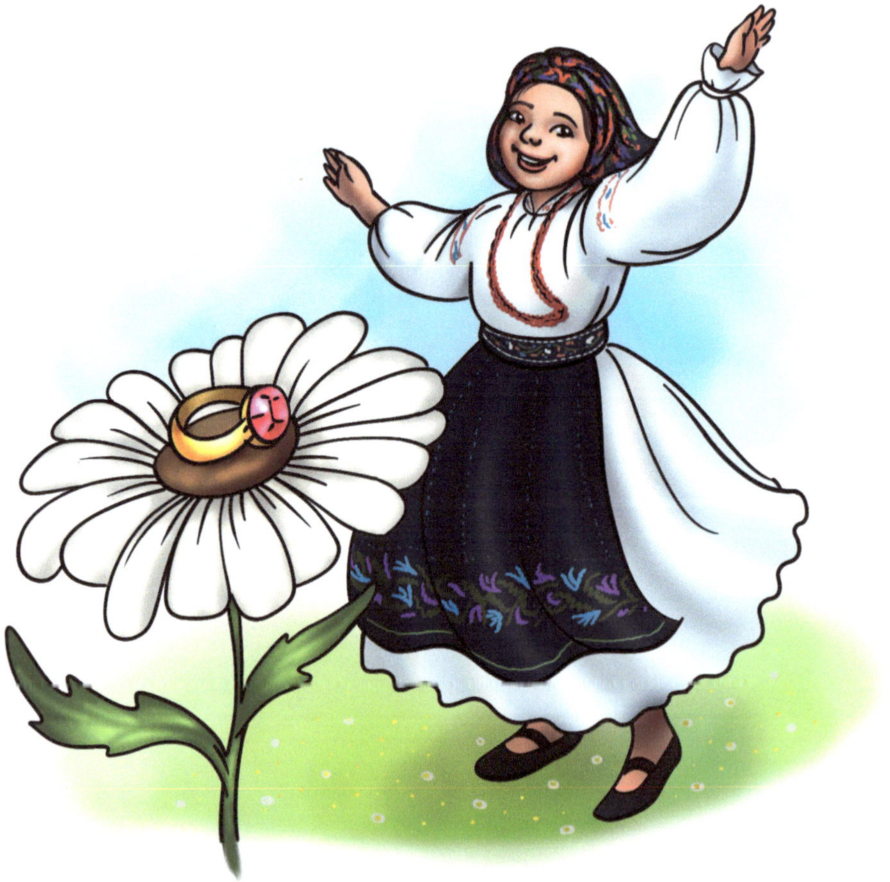

Romanian Princess Marie

Ss is for Sea Monster.

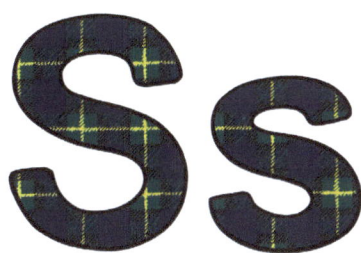

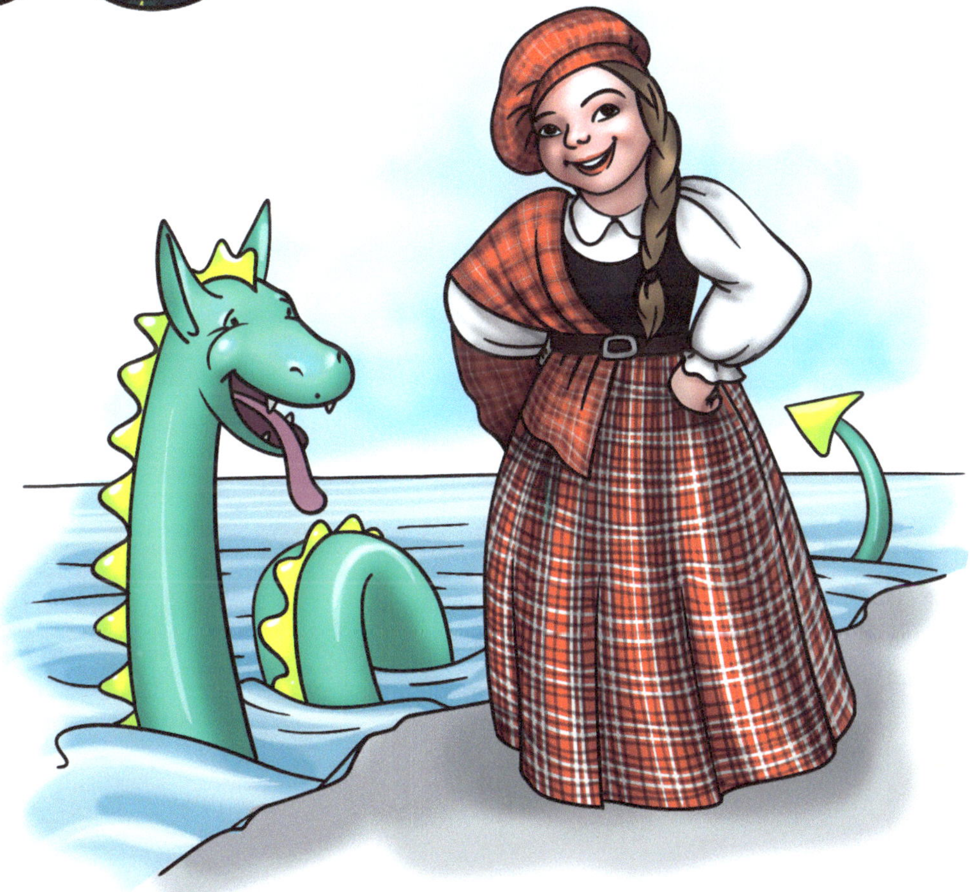

Scottish Princess Matilda

Tt is for Troll.

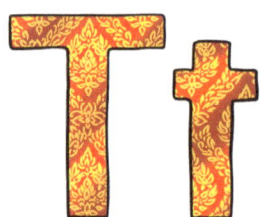

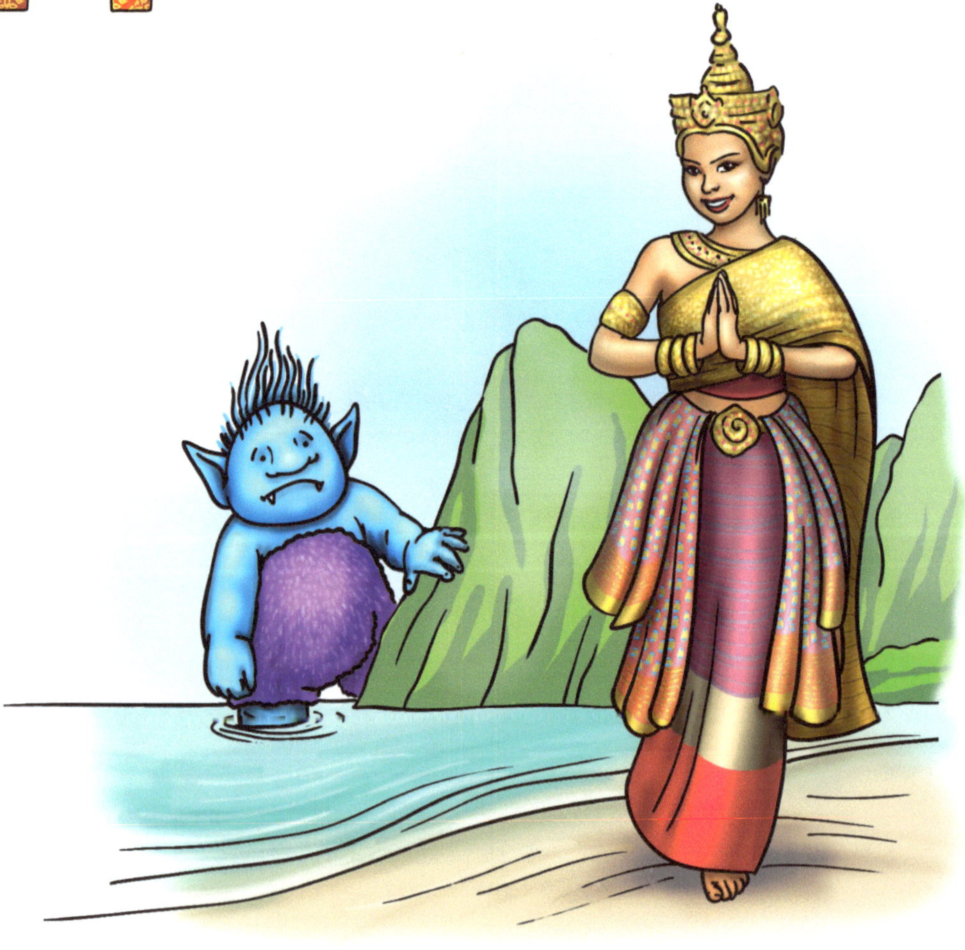

Thai Princess Saowapha

  is for Unicorn.

Ukrainian Princess Olha

Vv is for Village.

Vietnamese Princess Y Lan

Ww is for Warrior.

Welsh Princess Gwenllian

Xx is for eXplore.

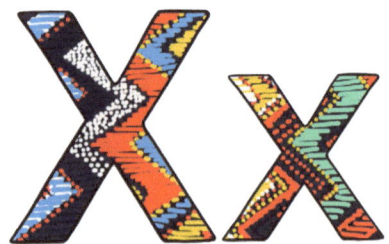

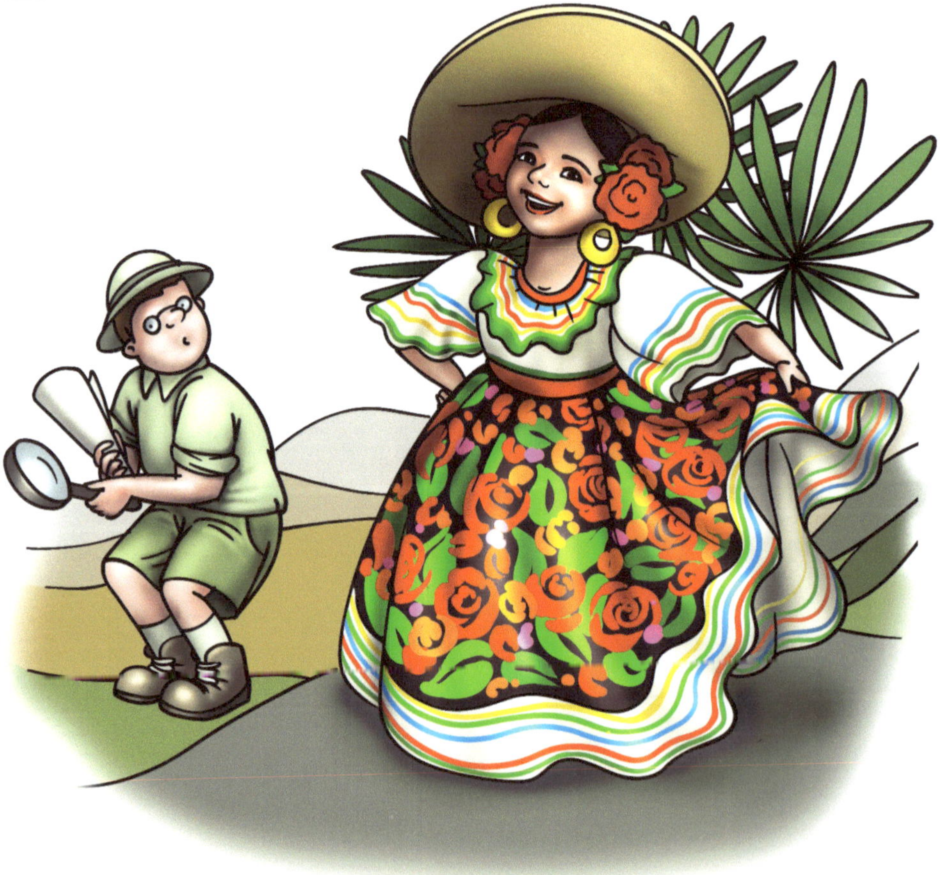

Mexican Princess Papantzin

Yy is for Yeti.

Yemeni Princess Asma

Learning Activities

Letter Sounds and Recognition
- On each page, point to the first letter. Identify the letter and sound (or sounds) it makes. Find the other words on the page that start with that letter.
- Point to the uppercase and lowercase letters.
- Come up with your own words that begin with each letter.
- Trace the letters at the end of the book.

Writing
- Practice writing each letter of the alphabet.
- Decorate your own letters of the alphabet.
- Write and illustrate your own Alphabet book using A is for _____. B is for _____. And so on.

Geography
- Look up the location of each princess' nationality or culture. Try to find pictures of that place.
- Which other countries start with each letter of the alphabet?

Cross-Cultural Connections
- Find more information about each nationality or culture listed in this book. What do you notice about them? How are they the same and different?
- Look up pictures of princesses from other cultures and countries.
- Discover the real people the princesses in this book are named for. You can find a summary of each at Heart-Soul-Mind.org in the free download titled, "Real International Princesses."

About the Author and Illustrator

Jenny Fulton is an award-winning author of children's books, a multi-genre author of a Bible study and YA fantasy book, and a freelance writer. In 2007, she received a B.S. in Bible, a B.S. in elementary education, and an endorsement in K-12 ESL from Grace University. Jenny has worked as a teacher in a variety of cultural and educational settings, both abroad and in the United States.

An enrolled member of the Navajo Nation, Jenny grew up in Kansas but regularly visited the reservations where she fell in love with the lands and its people. She currently resides in New Mexico with her husband and three creative, fantasy-loving daughters.

Olya (Olha) Tkachenko was born and got her formal education in Fine Arts in Ukraine. Since 2008 Olya worked as a freelance children's illustrator and graphic designer and created many children's books in the USA, Canada, and the UK. Olya's illustrations demonstrate her strong background in classic and folk art, with bright palettes, patterns, and decorative elements.

Currently, Olya and her husband live in Toronto. She leads a small company, Little Big Me, providing self-publishing authors with illustration and book design services.

www.ingramcontent.com/pod-product-compliance
Lightning Source LLC
Chambersburg PA
CBHW041436120626
46547CB00002B/245